SHARM EL-SHEIKH

SINAI AND THE RED SEA

WHITE STAR
PUBLISHERS

Sharm El-Sheikh
Sinai and the Red Sea

TEXTS
Fabrizio Calzia
Marco Maroccolo

GRAPHICS
Monica Morelli

TRANSLATION
Neil-Frazer Davenport

Contents

ISBN 88-8095-615-9

Reprints:
3 4 5 6 05 04 03

Printed in Italy

1
A Bedouin woman
displaying her traditional
costume.

2-3
The sea, the coral reef,
the desert: this is Ras
Mohamed, at a point
where the reef plunges into
the depths.

4-5
A panoramic view from
Gebel Musa at dawn.

6-7
An impressive, fiery red
group of alcyonarians or
soft corals.

9
A Bedouin woman in
ceremonial costume, her
face covered with a burqu,
a large cloth handkerchief
to which gold and brass
jewels and coins are
attached.

Introduction

The Sinai peninsula: the Asian region of Egypt. This vaguely triangular territory, 56,000 square kilometres, lies on the border between two continents; a confine traced by nature over 70 million years ago when Arabia began to break away from Africa, and one which man emphasised a century or so ago with the digging of the Suez Canal to link the Mediterranean and the Red Seas in order to favour maritime traffic and trade.

The Sinai peninsula: an arid and inhospitable world. Its landscape, sculpted by winds that have eroded rocky but friable mountains and carved canyons and passages in spectacular, warm-toned sandstones, transmits a wild and irresistible appeal. In the mutating light conditions at various times of the day, these natural sculptures with their remarkable forms take on the status of spontaneous works of art, offering a spectacle that endures until the last rays of the setting sun bathe them in a wondrous red glow.

Fertile land is at a premium here; the Nile flows along a parallel course at least a hundred kilometres to the west.

10 top and bottom
*Seen from a satellite, the
Sinai peninsula appears to
be an enormous triangle of
rock and sand, enclosed to
the east by the Gulf of*

*Aqaba, to the west by
the Gulf of Suez and to
the north by the
Mediterranean. In the
image above the course of
the Nile can be seen.*

11
*The Sinai is the product
of a geological process (the
separation of the continents)
that is still in progress.
In the picture, you can see*

*clearly the Gulf of Aqaba
above, Sharm el Sheikh
and Na'ama Bay in the
centre, the islands
of Tiran and Sanafir
at the right.*

12-13
A detail of the Ain Umm Ahmed Oasis.

12 bottom
A view of St. Catherine's Monastery.

Over the millennia, the river's placid waters have allowed the development of life-giving vegetation and the evolution of a great civilisation, but the Sinai was always, and remains, a desert region with its implications. Here it rains once every twenty years. The drying of its rivers has discouraged human settlement, making it at most a land of transit, an escape route, a strategic territory. And yet its bowels concealed, under a crust of granite and sandstone, unexpected treasures: as early as the Pharaonic and Roman times, gold, copper and turquoises were extracted from its mountains. Today, the mines have been abandoned: all that remain are hollowed out entrances, while the traces of ferrous oxide, sulphur and manganese lend further surprising brush-strokes of colour to the granite and sandstone crags. For the tourist, entering this land of a thousand and one colours signifies in the majority of cases undertaking a journey lasting a number of days away from the coast of the enchanting Red Sea, which the southern tip of Sinai divides into the Gulfs of Suez and Aqaba. The coastal region is a world diametrically opposed to that of the desert interior, a crystalline, limpid universe, a sea that dazzles with the pure blue reflections of the sky, striped by the

13 top
A Bedouin smoking a narghilè in his tent.

13 bottom
The sober colours of the fabric wrapped around the tomb of a Bedouin chieftain.

14

The coast in the Sharm el-Sheikh region alternates rock and sand lapped by crystalline waters.

14-15

Almost the entire coastline of the Ras Mohamed National Park, a true paradise for those who love the sea, is characterised by the presence of coral reefs.

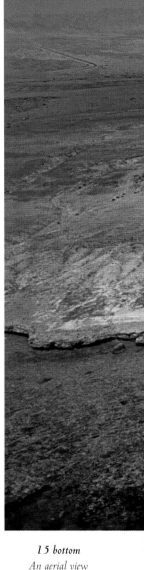

warm shading of the mountains mirrored in the waters and framing a landscape of beaches, palms and the self-contained white hotels that crowd the most well known resorts: Sharm el-Sheikh, Dahab, Nuweiba, the Ras Mohamed National Park, all names that echo around the world.

The true appeal of the Red Sea remains invisible from the surface. You need to immerse yourself in the water. A mask and a snorkel is all it takes to bring you into direct contact with a unique marine world, exuberant in the variety of its fauna, intriguing in the stunning design of its coral reefs, incredible in the chromatic surprises revealed in every square metre of sea. Your first dive to the reef of the Ras Mohamed National Park, beyond the southern tip of the Sinai peninsula, will regale you with incredible hues and schools of multi-coloured fish.

If those who go snorkelling will be stunned by the natural aquarium just below the surface, more experienced divers will be able to tackle greater depths beyond the reefs and explore secret, unexpected worlds and reach the wrecks of ships cloaked with brilliantly coloured living organisms.

The Red Sea, of course, also has its biblical connotations; its waters were parted to allow the passage of Moses and his people before sweeping away the pharaoh's soldiers. History or legend, faith or myth, prodigy or simple phenomenon of the seas, nothing stops the pilgrimage of divers from throughout the world who come here to take advantage of the numerous diving centres. And to discover that the promised land of the brochures, guidebooks, magazines and videos is a fabulous reality just waiting to be explored.

15 bottom
An aerial view of the Ras Mohamed National Park.

16-17
Na'ama Bay, with its huge tourist complexes.

18-19
A magnificent stretch of coastline near Taba.

20-21
The Beacon Rock reef where, in 1876, the British merchant ship Dunraven *was wrecked.*

—Sinai History—

The history of the Sinai, a harsh and ever inhospitable land, is above all a history of transit, a history of armies on the march, of peoples in flight, pilgrims travelling towards Mecca and incredulous crusaders. It is no coincidence that the story of the world's most famous Exodus, the one recorded in history with a capital "E", took place here, winding like a dramatic Ariadne's thread through an arid and baking labyrinth of canyons, impracticable passages, yawning chasms, dry, parched gorges and tracks erased by the wind and scorching heat.

For no less than forty years Moses and his people roamed this Dantean inferno: two and a half million Hebrews, a drifting army in search of a place in which to settle, condemned to live encamped in tents of goatskin, their belongings carried by asses, their children dragged on mats, the women and the flocks following on behind, in the hope of reaching the promised land that Yahweh finally indicated to a Moses exhausted by forty days of heat and silence on the summit of Gebel Musa.

How reliable are claims of the passage of Moses and the Hebrews along the route indicated by the Byzantine tradition? This is a question that has long engaged the interest of historians and explorers.

22 top left
A statue of Thutmosis III (1479-1425 BC) conserved in the Egyptian Museum of Cairo.

22 top right
A view of Pelusium (Pelousion), the present day Farama, the city the Romans considered to be the true "gateway to Egypt".

22 bottom left
The Navamis complex, where these circular, dry-stone tombs dating back to the Bronze Age were discovered.

22 bottom right
A statue of Mentuhotep III (2065-2014 BC) conserved in the Egyptian Museum of Cairo.

23
The temple of Serabit el-Khadim was built during the 12th Dynasty in an area in which the ancient pharaonic turquoise mines are concentrated.

The most recent and most reliable hypothesis actually suggests that the march took place much further to the north, from the Nile Delta in the direction of the Bitter Lakes (which would explain the bitter, undrinkable spring waters encountered by the Hebrews), and then across areas rich in pastureland and oases capable of feeding a fleeing population that was undoubtedly smaller than the three million quoted in the book of Exodus, but would nonetheless have probably numbered around 25,000. The tamarisk trees that produce manna are also much more common to the north. It should also be remembered that to the south the Hebrews would have come across the garrisons mounted by Ramses II to guard the copper and turquoise mines. Why run such a terrible and unnecessary risk? Lastly, the northern passage cuts horizontally across the Sinai peninsula and offers the most direct route to present-day Israel; that is to say, the Promised Land. Part of the patrimony of all humanity, testimony to this historical event lies in the rugged heart of the region,

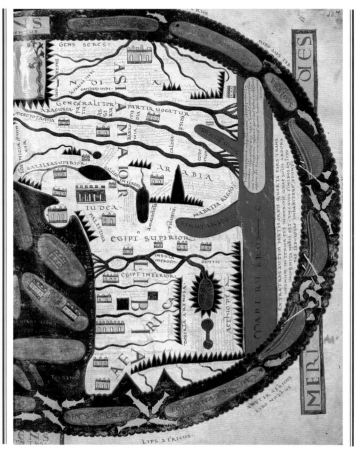

24 top
The Hereford Map drawn in 1290 by Richard of Haldingham, depicts the Red Sea in its "own" colour.

24 bottom
The Red Sea again, in a map drawn between 1042 and 1072 by the monk Gregory of San Severo and inspired by an 8th century map.

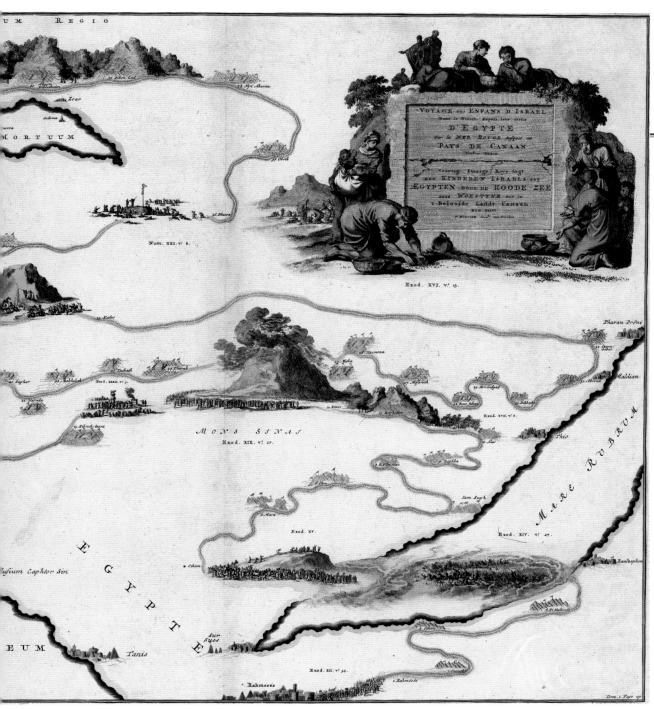

The map contains the following labels:

UM REGIO

MORTUUM

VOYAGE des ENFANS D'ISRAEL
Dans le Désert depuis leur sortie
D'EGYPTE
Par la MER ROUGE Jusques au
PAYS DE CANAAN
Nombre XXXIII.

Veertig Jaarige Reys togt
der KINDEREN ISRAELS uyt
ÆGYPTEN door de ROODE ZEE
door de WOESTYNE tot in
't Belooide Landt Canaan.
Num XXXIII.

Exod. XVI. v. 13.

MONS SINAI
Exod. XIX. v. 17.

MARE RUBRUM

Exod. XVII. v. 6.

Exod. XIV. v. 27.

Exod. XV.

Num. XXI. v. 1.

Exod. XIII. v. 34.

EGYPTE

Tanis

Rahmeses

where in the summer the thermometers soar above 50°C: up beyond the desert, St. Catherine's Monastery is home to a small community of orthodox monks, custodians of an archaic and in certain respects arcane religious culture that conserves the traces of the passage of Moses fleeing from Egypt towards the promised land. Here is the burning bush, a sign sent by God to the chosen people, and from here one can climb without undue difficulty to the summit of Gebel Musa, the Mountain of Moses, which at 2,285 metres overlooks the surrounding peaks as if it were the roof of the ideal and real world. Little does it matter that the highest peak in the Sinai is actually Gebel Katherina (2,637 metres); up here a

God going by the unpronounceable name of YHWH, or Yahweh, is said to have presented the leader of the Hebrew people with the tablets inscribed with the Ten Commandments, a *viaticum* for what was still a long trek, but above all a means of tranquillising his people, exhausted and assailed by doubt.

The flight of the Hebrews from Egypt was made possible by the crossing of the Red Sea which swept away their persecutors. This episode did not, however, discourage other armies at other times from attempting the same route. The Egyptians themselves made another assault centuries later under Thutmosis III, enjoying greater success as they went on to conquer Syria and Palestine. The

24-25

The Sinai as it appeared in 1690, in a print by P. Mortier: the biblical Exodus route is depicted, from Egypt to Palestine. According to the map and tradition, the Jews crossed the Red Sea south of Cairo, deviating towards Gebel Musa before heading to the Promised Land.

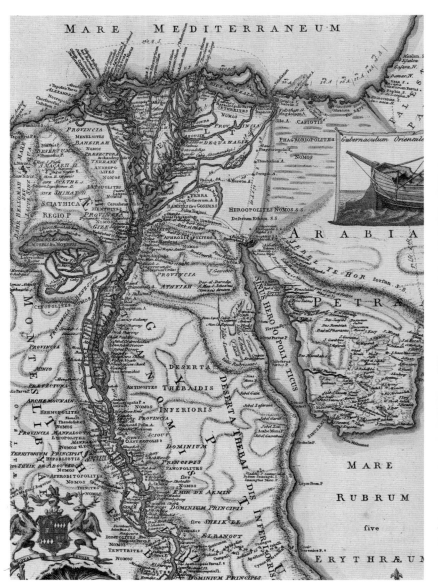

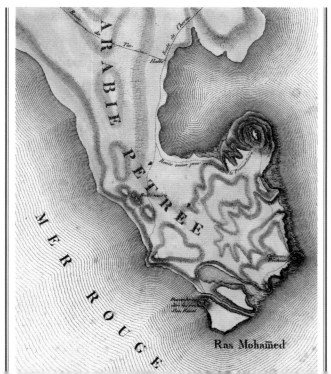

26 top
The Sinai, the Red Sea and the Nile delta in a 19th century map.

26 bottom
A highly detailed map taken from the book Voyage de l'Arabie Pétrée *by Léon de Laborde (1830) shows the Ras Mohamed peninsula.*

26-27
The Fortress of Aqaba, a plate taken from Léon de Laborde's Voyage de l'Arabie Pétrée.

return wave, in the form of Alexander the Great, was
to sweep away the Egyptians once again as the
Macedonian crossed the Sinai on his way to conquer
the land of the pharaohs. The course of history reveals
the traces of further passages, not least of which that
of the Romans. In 48 BC, the present-day Port Said
witnessed the conflict between the armies of Ptolemy
and his sister Cleopatra. The victory of the latter led
to her ascent to the throne of Egypt.

We then have to leap a number of centuries,
without losing track of the wider perspective: in 639
AD it was the turn of the troops of the Arab general
Amr to cross the Sinai on their way to conquer Egypt,
thus bringing a country rich in culture and tradition
into the fold of Islam. When the returning Christian
crusaders of the twelfth century threatened the
definitive reconquest of these lands, Saladin erected
the fortress of Qalat al-Gindi. The Sinai was
subsequently incorporated into the Ottoman empire

27 bottom
*The French artist and
traveller, Léon de Laborde,
in Oriental costume in a
drawing taken from*
Voyage de
l'Arabie
Pétrée.

28 top
*St. Catherine's Monastery
in a nineteenth century
plate by the Scottish artist,
David Roberts.*

28 bottom
*The Springs of Moses
depicted by David
Roberts.*

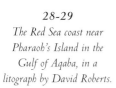

28-29
The Red Sea coast near
Pharaoh's Island in the
Gulf of Aqaba, in a
litograph by David Roberts.

29 bottom
The interior of St.
Catherine's Monastery, in a
drawing by David Roberts.

and then contested by the French and the British before the latter drew up the international boundary. The history of the twentieth century saw the Sinai make a dramatic return to the limelight: the Jewish people, who from these lands began their history of flight and dispersal across the centuries, a history blighted by persecution and culminating in the barbarities of the Nazi holocaust, rediscovered their homeland in Israel and along with it the primordial conflicts with the neighbouring peoples. In the meantime, the Sinai peninsula had acquired further strategic and commercial importance with the digging of the Suez canal which, when it opened in 1869, provided a miraculous passage between the Mediterranean and the Red Sea of almost biblical

significance. The so-called "Suez Crisis" of 1956, provoked by the decision of the Egyptian president Nassar to nationalise the canal, led to an invasion of the canal zone by Great Britain and France and induced Israeli troops to march into the Sinai.

The strong pressure brought to bear by the United Nations and the two superpowers, the USA and the USSR, re-established peace, but this was only the beginning of the Arab-Israeli conflict. In the June of 1967 the troops of General Sharon once again invaded the Sinai during the Six-Day War. The desert became the setting for bloody battles, its ancient silences fractured by the thunder of artillery-fire, the booming of mines and the hysterical, deadly coughing of machine guns. This time it was not the sacred fire of the God who presented himself to

Moses, who first indicated the path to be followed in the form of a burning bush before introducing a dialogue sanctified in the form of the Tables of the Law. A dramatic and pitiless guerrilla war was fought in these fragile mountains, the macabre traces of which still re-emerge from the fine desert sand today, almost as admonitory monuments to recent follies hurriedly expunged from the collective memory. Unexpected barriers spring up from nowhere marking an invisible line, the carcasses of tanks and armoured cars stand stark in the silence and blowing wind, fuel drums spout like hernias from a belly of rock and sand, almost mute tourist attractions from episodes experienced in black and white, transmitted throughout the world by the old evening television news programmes.

30 top
The opening of the Suez Canal in 1869, in a period print.

30-31
The Suez Canal as it was depicted in an idealised overhead view from the late nineteenth century.

31 top
Israeli military exercises in the Sinai, following the Yom Kippur War.

31 centre
A photo from the Six-Day War fought in 1967.

31 bottom left
The Suez Crisis, 1956: military operations in the contested Sinai peninsula.

31 bottom right
This photo from the 1960s shows an Israeli naval vessel patrolling the Gulf of Aqaba.

— The Bedouins —

The Bedouins are nomadic herders many of whom have, over time, become virtually sedentary. The only people to have inhabited these arid lands almost from time immemorial, the Bedouins of the Sinai comprise around a dozen tribes with a total population of approximately 50,000.

While it is true that herding remains one of their principal resources, with the women and children designated for the heaviest labours, the irksome tourist invasion has actually opened up new avenues for these people. The few that have remained now survive thanks to these new opportunities: the once nomadic tribes now live here in the precious shade of the palms, earning a crust as tour guides or by opening their homes to

32 top
Bedouins sifting the sand in an oasis in search of precious minerals.

32 centre
Water replenishment in the north of the Sinai.

32 bottom
A Bedouin woman leads her camel along a track.

33
A group of Bedouins riding camels. Their name derives from bedu, *which means "inhabitant of the desert".*

curious visitors eager to snap yet more photographs.

Some of the Bedouins station themselves along the steep footpaths that climb Gebel Musa or Gebel Katherina, the Sinai's highest mountains, in order to offer cups of tea to the exhausted excursionists. Others offer camel riding trips and almost all live in camps composed of large tents pitched within oases that shelter them from the mountainous desert, or in the vicinity of tourist resorts such as Dahab and Nuweiba.

The tourists staying in the villages along the coast may enjoy alternating the sea and sand with excursions into the dunes and canyons, perhaps on camels. They may stop in a Bedouin village where they could enjoy a warm supper around a living fire lit to ward off the cold of the precocious desert night. They will also be able to admire and acquire examples of Bedouin crafts, including the highly colourful women's clothing.

34 top left
A Bedouin woman gathering wild herbs among the desert dunes.

34 bottom left
A young unmarried Bedouin girl may leave her face uncovered.

34 bottom right
The typical head-dress worn by Bedouin men is called a kafia, a triangle of white fabric.

35
This Bedouin woman has her face semi-concealed by a red burqu.

36-37
Bedouin women herding in Central Sinai.

36 bottom
A Bedouin encampment near Taba, on the shores of the Red Sea.

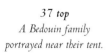

37 top
A Bedouin family
portrayed near their tent.

37
A typical Bedouin
encampment in Central
Sinai.

38-39
Preparing the evening meal
in a Bedouin encampment.

Taba and the surrounding area

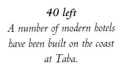

For those arriving from Israel, Taba represents their first encounter with the Sinai peninsula.

The frontier coastal town can actually be reached on foot from Eilat (thanks to an agreement between the two countries special two-week visas are issued). An area contested during the Egyptian-Israeli war, Taba was only restored to Egypt as recently as 1989.

Since then projects have been set up to develop the town as a tourist resort capable of competing with Eilat.

Taba already boasts one luxury hotel, a number of other large hotels, good restaurants on the sea front specialising in exquisitely fresh fish, bars and cafés, and, above all, a broad, sandy beach that extends in front of a backdrop of rugged mountains and guarantees a pleasant, relaxing stay.

For those arriving from Egypt, moreover, Taba offers a full range of opportunities for day trips or longer excursions into the Sinai.

For example, taxis depart from here, running first along the coastal road before crossing the dramatic desert scenery further inland, and reach St. Catherine's Monastery in a couple of hours.

40 left
A number of modern hotels have been built on the coast at Taba.

40 right
The reflections of the
sunset tinge the coral sea
orange.

40-41
The "Fjord", a suggestive
bay on the coast between
Taba and Nuweiba.

41 bottom and 42-43
Pharaoh's Island is located
just off Taba. It is also
known as Gezirea el-
Faraun or Coral Island.
The Crusader castle built
in the 12th century can be
seen on the summit.

Nuweiba

85 kilometres north of Dahab lies the port and tourist resort of Nuweiba, an urban conglomerate extending along the delta of the Wadi Watir.

For centuries, Nuweiba was a significant stop on the pilgrim route to Mecca. The town is divided into two parts, separated by an 18th century Turkish citadel. Each of the two quarters possesses its own distinct character: to the south, along the shores of the bay, is the port of Muzeina – a fishing village – with fabulous beaches and coral reefs, while to the north, in the area furthest from the tongue of land that protrudes into the Gulf of 'Aqaba to form the bay, a collection of numerous tourist villages known as Nuweiba el-Tarabin, has been built. Of note in this area are the ruins of a stronghold constructed in the early 16th century by the Mameluke

sultan, Ashraf Qqnsouh el-Ghouri, to defend the Sinai from Turkish invasion, thus guaranteeing the safety of travellers who found themselves in the vicinity of the city's port. Over the centuries, the fortress proved an inadequate obstacle to Turkish expansion and was slowly relegated to the rank of a staging-post with ample supplies of fresh water for the Bedouins.

In spite of its beautiful beach, Tarabin, close to which a number of Bedouin tribes still live, is less intensively developed than Muzeina.

Apart from dives in its splendid waters, Nuweiba also offers its visitors excursions aboard camels or off-road vehicles to the nearby Coloured Canyon or the small Ain el-Furtaga oasis, as well as extraordinary scenery which you can admire along the road between Nuweiba and Taba.

44
The magnificent beach at Nuweiba stretches between El-Tarabin and Muzeina.

44-45
A suggestive view of the coast at Nuweiba.

45 bottom left
The Mameluke fortress of Ashraf el-Ghuri, at Nuweiba el-Tarabin, was erected in the 16th century to protect the passing caravans. It was restored during the Ottoman period.

45 bottom right
*The palms, drawing
on subterranean spring
water, reach the beach
to Nuweiba.*

46-47
*Behind the inhabited area, a
narrow tongue of sand separates
Nuweiba from the wadis heading
inland towards central Sinai.*

Dahab

From Sharm el-Sheik it takes about 45 minutes to reach Dahab, situated some 80 km south of Nuweiba. The route passes through unforgettable scenery: against the backdrop of the Sinai mountains you encounter oases still inhabited by the Bedouins and fabulous canyons boasting a stunning range of colours. A fork in the road is followed by the town of Dahab, whose name means "gold". You should harbour no illusions, however: the deep yellow tones of the sand reveal the origin of the name. The magic word in this area is instead "tourism", thanks to the discovery of the wonders of the coral reef.

The old Bedouin village of Assalah, set in a palm grove and overlooking a fantastic bay, is today enlivened by a significant number of bars, restaurants, shops and hotels. Assalah is now the most intensively developed part of town; the administrative centre is located in Dahab itself.

The shallows of Dahab can be reached directly from the shore and offer unique and spectacular

48 top
The Bay of Qura, protected from the sea but exposed to the wind, is an ideal place for windsurfing.

48 bottom
The village of Assalah has expanded rapidly in recent years.

48-49
In the Bedouin language, the place-name Dahab means "gold", the colour of the sands on these beaches.

dive sites. The dives in the area are characterised by the canyons which make this stretch of sea so special. A canyon, easily reached from the coastal road heading north, actually gives its name to one of the divers' favourite spots. At a depth of around 15 metres, coral formations act as an introduction to the site's main attraction, a cavern plunging to a depth of 50 metres that offers an exit on the external wall of the reef.

Another stunning dive site is Blue Hole, a vertical cavity that can be swum to from Assalah and which again reaches a depth of 50 metres. The spectacle of the internal walls carpeted with sponges and stoney coral formations is exalted by the play of sunlight which magically penetrates the cavern.

49 bottom and 50-51
The Dahab promontory closes hook-like around the Bay of Qura, dividing from that of Ghazala. The sea presents turquoise highlights, evidence of the presence of an interesting coral reef.

52-53
The village of Assalah, at Dahab, is one of the most picturesque sites, beloved by tourists searching for local character.

Nabq
—— and ——
Ras Abu Gallum

Located around 25 kilometres north of Sharm el-Sheikh, the Nabq Reserve presents a significant variety of natural environments: from the inland mountains to the dunes in the south and the rich area of coral where the desert meets the sea. The interior is characterised by the presence of a number of wadis, dry for much of the year, but capable of supporting the Bedouin tribes and their flocks thanks to the occasional but heavy rains.

The varied mineral composition of the mountains in this area is interesting from the points of view of both geology and the scenery it produces. The desert zone, characterised by three different dune systems, is instead closed to the public. The shoreline has a wealth of coral communities and is home to a notable variety of fish species.

The local Bedouin population, concentrated in the villages of Kheriza and Ghargana can be seen as an integral part of the very landscape. Traditionally dedicated to fishing, the Bedouins now also offer tourist services such as camel excursions.

Like Nabq, the Ras Abu Gallum Reserve is part of the overall programme of nature

54 top
The Mangrove Forest in the Nabq Reserve.

54 bottom
Mangroves have found an ideal habitat in the Nabq Reserve.

54-55
A carpet of mangrove roots.
In the distance can seen the
wreck of the Maria
Schroeder which ran
aground in the shallows in
1965.

55 bottom and 56-57
A superb coral reel, of
impressive dimensions,
barely covered by the waters
of the Nabq Reserve.

58 top and 58-59
In the Ras Abu Gallum
Reserve the rocks appear to
plunge into the transparent
waters of the Red Sea.

preservation planned by the authorities of the Ras Mohamed National Park. It is still naturally wild, being both far from the traditional tourist destinations and of strategic importance and therefore of military interest. Recently, the significance of the area to the maintenance of the Sinai's environmental equilibrium has been recognised, along with its importance to the Bedouin tribes who live here and base their economy above all on the exploitation of its fish stocks. Characterised by spectacular granite mountains that plunge sheer to its beaches, Abu Gallum is distinguished by its rich and varied ecosystems as well as its coral reefs. In this area 167 desert plant species have been identified, some of which are not found in the neighbouring Ras Mohammed and Nabq reserves.

Of equal interest is the presence of mammals such as the red fox and the striped hyena and reptiles such as the fearsome black cobra. Route, dive sites and the Bedouin fishing reserves are all well indicated so as to safeguard the protected area.

58 bottom
Many Bedouins still fish for a living in the Ras Abu Gallum Reserve.

59 bottom
A fisherman's hut has been built using some of the large shells scattered along the beach.

The Strait of Tiran

60

The Strait of Tiran closes the Gulf of Aqaba to the south and represents, with its fabulous reefs, one of the divers' favourite haunts.

60-61

Gordon reef is the southernmost of the four reefs aligned in the Strait of Tiran.

61 bottom

The waves break on the Ras Nasrani reef off the coast of Sharm el-Sheikh, the home of a pulsating submarine life.

The Strait of Tiran is the western equivalent of the Strait of Gubal and constitutes the access route from the "open" Red Sea to the Gulf of 'Aqaba. It takes its name from the volcanic island of Tiran which drastically narrows the available channel for the passage of boats. As if this were not enough, vessels passing through this area are obliged to negotiate four extensive coral reefs rising from a depth of over one thousand metres. Navigation is still further complicated by the strong currents. These same currents do, however, play a vital role in the local ecosystem, as they carry into the area a vast quantity of plankton which is highly attractive to

numerous marine species. This helps create the ideal environment for an abundant flora and fauna. An exceptional underwater world is out there waiting to be discovered, although the strong currents and considerable depths do mean that this is an area for prudent and experienced divers.

Ras Nasrany is the westernmost promontory of the strait's southern extremity: a tongue of land composed of steep coral walls that descend to a depth of over 100 metres, interrupted for stretches by ledges of stoney coral.

The external edge of the reef presents complex black coral structures, whilst at a depth of fifteen metres, fantastic coral formations and sea-fans are

62, 63 and 64-65
The island of Tiran is situated in the centre of the strait, flanked to the east by the small island of Sanafir. The two islands have played significant strategic and military roles. But, as demonstrated in these photos, they are also of considerable naturalistic interest, with the whole of the island of Tiran having been annexed by the Ras Mohamed National Park. The natural beauty of the four coral reefs extending along the strait (Gordon, Jackson, Thomas and Woodhouse Reefs) has made them favourite destinations for the divers of Na'ama Bay.

to be found. The seabed is enlivened by the spectacular presence of small, brilliantly coloured fish, large groupers and turtles. At 30-40 metres, the reef forms a sharp step and drops towards the abysses. Gordon Reef is the southernmost point of the Strait of Tiran coral formation.

On the southern side, the seabed presents a broad sandy plain at a depth of around 15-20 metres, with perfectly intact and highly ramified stoney coral structures. A further broad sandy hollow extends at around 20 metres and is often frequented by whitetip reef sharks. The northern side of the reef can only be explored in optimal weather and sea conditions and it is here that you may see, among other species, more sharks and turtles.

Thomas Reef is the smallest of the four pinnacles that rise from the seabed. It is located in an area of strong currents that restrict dives and prevent a complete tour of the pinnacle itself. The southern side offers views of magnificent corals and a great variety of fish.

Located a short distance north of Thomas Reef, Woodhouse Reef is narrow and elongated in form. At a depth of around 40 metres, the eastern side features a coral wall that rises parallel to that of Woodhouse, creating a deep, narrow canyon. At 20 metres a sandy plain houses black corals and sea-fans. In this area of sea it is not unusual to encounter leopard and whitetip reef sharks.

Circular in shape, Jackson Reef is the northernmost in the Strait of Tiran located around two and a half kilometres off the island of Tiran. At a depth of around 30 metres, the reef presents numerous crevices which offer shelter to groupers and many other species.

67 top
The wreck of the Maria Schroeder, *as it appeared in 1975, ten years after she ran aground on the reef a few metres from the beach at Nabq.*

67 centre
This skeleton now devoured by the salt water, is what remains of the Maria Schroeder *today, over three and a half decades after the incident.*

66
Seen from above, the Red Sea reveals the notable extension of its coral reefs, the habitat of thousands of marine species. These reefs, sharp and barely covered by the water, have frequently proved fatal for the boats that sail these waters. It is by no means rare to see wrecks, testimony to disasters and tragedy. In this photo you can see the wreck of the Hedoroma Million Hope, *which ran aground off the oasis of Nabq.*

67 bottom
The cargo ship Louillia *struck the stoney coral structure of Gordon Reef and listed onto one side, but the reef then prevented her from sinking.*

Sharm el-Sheikh and Na'ama Bay

Today considered to be one of the world's most popular diving resorts, up to the first half of the 1980s, Sharm el-Sheikh was a quiet fishing village inhabited by Bedouins free to enjoy in absolute tranquillity a paradise of turquoise waters framed by the burning ochre of the mountains; in truth, the tourist development of the "Bay of the Sheikh" (to translate its name from the local language) had begun in the late Seventies, during the Israeli occupation. In just a few decades, the face of Sharm el-Sheikh has changed radically: imposing, ultra-modern hotels have been built along the coast, complete with swimming pools, sun-beds and parasols.

68 top
The tourist port of Sharm el-Sheikh has seen the number of recreational boats increase over the years.

68 bottom
Ras Umm Sid is the promontory that closes the Bay of Sharm el-Sheikh. The el-Fanar (Lighthouse) restaurant can be seen here.

68-69
The village of Sharm el-Sheikh has grown in importance over the years thanks to tourism, but it has retained its original characteristics as a fishing village and natural harbour.

69 bottom
The tourist complexes of Sharm el-Sheikh have developed on the tongue of land the Sharm el-Maya to the east.

70 and 71

*Na'ama Bay, located
a few kilometres north of
Sharm el-Sheikh, has
witnessed remarkable
development; large,
modern hotel complexes*
*have been erected on the
beautiful beaches of the
Red Sea, making this
village overlooking Mersa
el-At the most important
tourist resort in the
southern Sinai.*

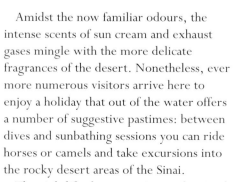

Amidst the now familiar odours, the
intense scents of sun cream and exhaust
gases mingle with the more delicate
fragrances of the desert. Nonetheless, ever
more numerous visitors arrive here to
enjoy a holiday that out of the water offers
a number of suggestive pastimes: between
dives and sunbathing sessions you can ride
horses or camels and take excursions into
the rocky desert areas of the Sinai.

The nightlife also now mirrors the rituals
typical of the West: from restaurants to
night clubs, from discotheques to small
bars, everything is organised so that the
tourists, perhaps thousands of kilometres
from home, feel perfectly at ease.

A natural prolongation of Sharm el-
Sheikh, the stunning Na'ama Bay is located
on the stretch of coastline that reaches Wadi
al-Aat.

The resort boasts a number of attractions
and offers some of the Sinai's most
suggestive underwater itineraries.

Na'ama Bay has only relatively recently

begun to attract tourists: in terms of accommodation it offers a reasonable number of hotels and shops and a stimulating nightlife, made-to-measure for western visitors.

A dive in the waters off the area comprising Sharm el-Sheikh and Na'ama Bay offers the opportunity of coming into contact with the enchanted and uncontaminated world of the Red Sea coral reefs.

Even novice divers can, taking the usual precautions, descend to the seabed in this area, where the waters are sheltered from the currents by the coral formations, and discover its marvel for themselves. Numerous diving centres offer accelerated courses: just a few days is all it takes to obtain a certificate that gives you the right to dive to interesting depths equipped with scuba gear and accompanied by instructors. There are also dozens of boats that every day carry divers to the most famous dive sites not far from the coast.

72 top
Shark Bay, a few kilometres north of Na'ama Bay, still boasts corners of unspoilt beauty.

72 centre
An internal road in Na'ama Bay tourist complex.

72 bottom
The Tower Hotel and the Sharm Club overlook Tower Bay, between Sharm el-Sheikh and Na'ama.

72-73
Immense and luxurious hotel structures have allowed Na'ama Bay to attract the interest of international mass tourism.

73 bottom
The attractive and imposing Sofitel hotel complex, to the north of Na'ama Bay.

74-75

The coastal resorts of
Sharm el-Sheikh and
Na'ama Bay have now
acquired world-wide fame
and are appropriately
equipped to welcome
tourists and divers from all
over the globe. The
numerous large hotels
provide hospitality for

hundreds of thousands of
visitors each year, the
diving centres offer
assistance and equipment
for those who intend
to dive in the waters
of the Red Sea and
explore an unspoilt
and brilliantly
colourful world.
This photo shows the

Sheikh Coast Coral Bay
Hotel, one of the most
modern in the area.
Unmistakable for its
extensive and luxuriant
gardens, it overlooks
the bay of the same name,
an enchanting stretch
of sea characterised
by a magnificent
coral reef.

75 top

Even in such an arid land,
thanks to the work
of local operators, a golf
course has been created
within the Mövenpick
Golf Resort, a further
attraction for those staying
in the Sharm el-Sheikh-
Na'ama Bay tourist
district.

75 centre
*The Hyatt Regency, with
its original terraced
swimming pools, is located
to the north of Na'ama.*

75 bottom
*The unmistakable semicircle
that characterises the
Mövenpick Resort, a stone's
throw from the reef.*

76-77
The Ras Mohamed promontory is a tongue of land that contrasts strongly with the deep blue of the sea.

76 bottom left
The Mangrove Channel separates the island of the same name from Ras Mohamed and the mainland.

76 bottom right
The rocky walls falling sheer to the sea at Marsa Bareika continue below the surface, almost reaching the coral reef.

77
Ras Mohamed and Main Beach extend towards the sea. Here can be seen the Shark Observatory and Jolanda and Shark Reefs, diving paradises.

Ras Mohamed

Ras Mohamed is located on the southern tip of the Sinai peninsula, almost marking the confine between the gulfs of Suez and 'Aqaba.

In 1983, this narrow promontory composed of fossilised coral was incorporated within the Ras Mohamed National Park which comprises the whole of the coral reef structure off the Sinai's

root patterns also retain numerous sediments and enrich the waters. Numerous species of birds find ideal nesting sites in the roots of these plants.

The terrestrial areas of the park also appear to have once belonged to the submarine world: out of the great dunes to the north of the promontory emerge calcareous formations that date back to

78-79
Jackfish Alley bay at Ras Mohamed is embraced by fossilised coral rocks that emerged around 70,000 years ago.

80-81
From above it is possible to appreciate in full the unusual shape of the Ras Mohamed promontory, extending into the coral sea like an open hand. In this photo Hidden Bay and the Mangrove Channel can also be seen.

southern coast. The reserve initially covered 97 square kilometres, while today it extends over 480 and also embraces the islands of Tiran and Sanafir and the coral reef around Sharm el-Sheikh.

The Ras Mohamed National Park also comprises and protects the inland areas characterised by unusual ecosystems such as the coastal dunes and the mangrove swamps.

The latter are characteristic of the Indian Ocean and develop here at the northern extremity of their area. The mangroves stabilising of the sandy bottoms and the coastline is crucial: their aerial roots filter the sea water and then expel it, guaranteeing a continuous exchange of oxygen. Their intricate

the Miocene epoch and contain a rich variety of marine fossils.

The coastal areas instead represent an ideal habitat for a number of animals such as foxes, gazelles, ibexes and hyenas and birds such as white and black storks and grey herons.

The coming and going of tourists obliges the fauna to hide during the day, but with a little luck it is possible to spot some species, especially in the early hours of the morning.

The marine fauna displays greater variety: in the shallows of the coastal area, favoured by the specific conditions of transparency and temperature, live around 150 different pelagic species.

82 top
The Mangrove Channel cuts through the rocks and reef of Ras Mohamed, creating the island of the same name.

82 bottom
The theatrical entrance to the Ras Mohamed National Park in reinforced concrete is the work of an Egyptian artist.

83 top
It is by no means rare to encounter examples of desert foxes (the species Vulpes rueppelli, *and* Vulpes zenda) *in the Ras Mohamed National Park.*

83 centre
A desert fox running along the beach at Ras Mohamed. The park's terrestrial fauna also includes gazelles, wild goats and small rodents.

The sun-drenched and dazzling coral platform of Ras Mohamed gives no indication that just a few metres beyond the promontory, the sea floor plunges almost sheer to a depth of 600 metres. Not far from the same stretch of coast, however two majestic stoney coral pinnacles rise from the seabed and graze the surface.

These are Shark and Jolanda Reefs, the park's two main underwater attractions.

The two colossal coral towers are linked by a saddle of sand that lies at a depth of no more than 20 metres. In this area you may observe the passage of large fish such as tuna, barracudas and Teira batfish *(Platax teira)* which brave the strong currents.

Jolanda Reef, the largest of the coralline towers, took its name from a merchant vessel wrecked here in 1981.

The reef has incorporated some of the remains of the wreck within its structure and they have

been colonised by fantastic corals. Among the most popular dives, of particular note is the one that visits the Shark Observatory. Here you may see those pelagic fish that have been driven away from Sharm el-Sheikh by the constant presence of divers. The area is populated by barracudas, sea bream and tuna.

The Anemone City area, a sandy plain between Shark Reef and the barrier reef is particularly suggestive: the anemones which flourish in the area accompanied by the faithful clownfish may reach up to a metre in diameter.

83 bottom
A colony of storks
(Ciconia ciconia):
around 20,000
examples of this species
stop over in the Ras
Mohamed National
Park during their
annual migration.

The Red Sea

This long and narrow strip of sea of an intense blue contrasts strongly with the dazzling yellow of the surrounding terrain composed of arid mountains and sandy deserts. Seen from above, the Red Sea is a chromatic prelude to the wonders of its rich depths, teaming with fish and corals of myriad species and colours. And yet, in the depths of its abysses, this natural paradise conceals dramatic origins: its waters fill a tectonic fracture dating back millions of years, a fracture that gave rise to the continents of Asia and Africa. The process of separation is still in progress: the Egyptian shore continues to draw away from its Arabian counterpart by 2 cm a year. At this rate, the Red Sea will become an ocean within another 150 million years, or so the experts say and who are we to contradict them.

It is easier to stick to the present day dimensions: the Red Sea is no more than 350 kilometres wide but almost 2,300 kilometres long. These statistics have only a relative importance: the true beauty of this sea lies in the extreme depths of abysses which in the Gulf of Aqaba, that is to say the area of greatest interest to tourists and the richest in fauna, reach 1,400 metres. These immense depths are the result of another vast crack in the earth's crust, the Syrian-African fault between the continental plates of Asia and Africa which affects the course of the River Jordan, the Dead Sea and, in fact, the Gulf of Aqaba. Of the three broad levels of depth that characterise the Red Sea, the one of greatest interest to tourists descends to 50 metres at a distance of at most 12 and a half kilometres offshore and offers a submarine environment rich in, above all, corals. Who could ever suspect that such marvels exist so close to barren shores preceding arid mountains that themselves conceal inhospitable inland deserts?

To what does the Red Sea owe its name? It is difficult to arrive at the undoubtedly ancient origins of the definition. It appears, in fact, that the Phoenicians had already attributed this chromatic peculiarity to its waters.

The Romans, Latinizing the Greek name, defined it as "erythraeum"; that is to say "red", a colour they associated with the south.

The Egyptians instead spoke of Wasi-Wr, that is, the "Green Expanse", sticking closer to the true colour of the water with its wonderful emerald reflections.

According to other hypotheses, the name derives from the blooms of Trichodesmium erythraeum, an algae which releases a red colouring to the surface of the water when it dies off. Then there are the corals. In their period of reproduction, they release thousands of tiny pink eggs into the water.

84 top
In the fantastic underwater world of the Red Sea, lavishly coloured groups of sea-fans and fish of all sizes, shapes and hues guarantee a fabulous and ever-changing scenario. This photo shows a coral grouper (Cephalopholis miniata).

84 bottom
A squirrelfish (Sargocentron sp.) swims amidst the stoney coral formations.

85
Soft corals and sea-fans flourish in the warm waters of the Red Sea.

86-87
A scorpionfish (Pterois volitans) *circling on the reef.*

86 bottom
A coral grouper (Cephalopholis miniata) *emerging from a crevice densely colonised by madrepores and soft corals.*

87 top
A number of particularly well developed sea-fans.

87 centre
The striped clownfish (Amphiprion bicinctus) *lives in symbiosis with the sea anemone.*

87 bottom
The parrotfish (Scarus gibbus) *can reach up to 70 centimetres in length.*

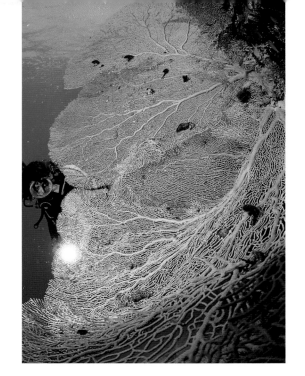

The most historically reliable version is associated with the wonderful city of Petra, carved into the red sandstone of the Jordan desert. The city's first inhabitants were called the Edomites (from the Hebrew term edom meaning "red"). Their territory extended as far as the Gulf of Aqaba, an obligatory point of embarkation for Jews trading with the south. Later, when the Nabataeans had replaced the Edomites, the ancient world continued to define that point of embarkation, and by extension the whole area of sea as far as the Indian Ocean, as "red".

Quite apart from its intriguing name, the depth of its central trenches makes the Red Sea unique: down at the bottom of the abysses, the lava that rises from the earth's mantle warms the water to

88-89
The forest-like colonies of the soft-corals tend to cloak the walls of the reef.

88 bottom left
Clouds of glassfish swim through the coral formations.

88 bottom right
A group of masked butterflyfish (Chaetodon semilarvatus). This is a species typical of the Red Sea.

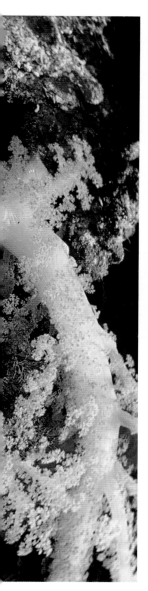

89 top
A school of soldierfish
(Myripristis murdjan)
*speeding through the deep
blue of the sea off Sharm el-
Sheikh.*

90-91
The Napoleon wrasse
(Cheilinus undulatus),
*here flanked by a jack,
may weigh up to 180
kilogrammes.*

the point that even at a depth of 300 metres the average temperature is around 20° C. In these ideal conditions marine fauna naturally flourishes. The incredible variety of coral formations and the virtually unlimited wealth of fish species (thousands of different types of fish have been identified in these waters), makes the shallows of the Red Sea a unique spectacle. It is of guaranteed interest from a strictly biological point of view, but also of such dramatic visual impact as to attract divers from throughout the world. It would be impossible to list all the species present in these waters, but they include abundant and brilliantly coloured reef fish, the crocodile fish, the porcupine fish, butterfly fish, sea turtles, rays, stingrays, moray eels, sea-fans and soft corals. This stunning array enlivens an intense experience that is renewed on each dive, metre by metre.

Another characteristic feature of the area and one favoured by divers, is the presence of wrecks of the many boats that criss-crossed seas which had been made treacherous by the sharp coral reefs just below the surface, especially

prior to the cutting of the Suez Canal. The most dangerous area was considered to be that of the islands in the Strait of Gubal: these waters, in fact, conceal the remains of numerous ships that have sunk over the centuries. Among the most interesting wrecks to visit, for those with diving experience, are two ships of different types but similar destinies that lie off the Gubal islands.

The British merchant ship *Ulysses* sank, it is thought, in 1887. She lies at a depth of 25 metres, close to the promontory of Bluff Point. The ship was identified from a plate from thr board dinner service.

At a depth of 10 metres, lying on the sandy bottom at the heart of southern bay of Gubal, are the remains of a small Egyptian vessel which was probably used as a patrol boat during the Six-Day War. Its heavily corroded interior provides a refuge for small reef fish and stupendous Spanish dancers *(Hexabranchus sanguineus)*.

The keel, in contact with the seabed, forms numerous crevices which have now become ideal habitats for large moray eels and sea urchins.

92 top
*A school of black-finned
barracudas (*Sphyraena
qenie*).*

92 bottom
*A whitetip reef shark
(*Carcharhinus
wheeleri*) roaming
solitary in the open sea.*

92-93
An encounter with dolphins (Tursiops tursiops) *is always a joyful occasion for divers.*

93 bottom
The majestic flight of a manta ray (Manta birostris), *accompanied by a number of remoras.*

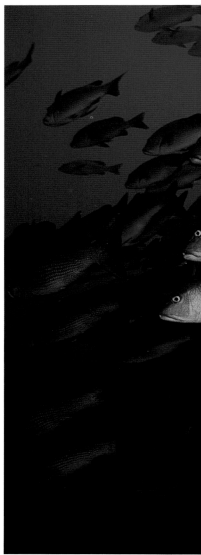

94 top
The unmistakable profile of hammerhead sharks
(Sphyrna lewini).

94 bottom
A school of jacks (Caranx sexfasciatus) *swimming in formation.*

94-95
During the summer months thousands of examples of the red snapper congregate at Shark Reef (Lutjanus bohar).

95 bottom
During a dive in the Red Sea it is not infrequent to encounter a sea turtle (Chelonia midas).

Considering the dangers of the reefs around the islands in the Strait of Gubal, other boats chose to sail at a prudent distance off the western shore of the Sinai, beyond Ras Mohamed. Some of these were no more fortunate, however, as here too the barely submerged reefs proved fatal. Thus did the British merchant ship *Dunraven* come to grief in 1876, when she struck Beacon Rock. The consequent fire broke the ship into two sections. The wreck was found in 1979 at a depth of 28 metres. At the stern, the propeller and rudder are adorned with soft corals and sponges, whilst the engine room and the boiler can be seen inside.

Not far from the *Dunraven*, in the vicinity of the Sha'ab Ali reef, lies the wreck of the Thistlegorm, a merchant ship laden with arms that was sailing through this area in October, 1941. This time, however, the coral reefs had nothing to do with the disaster. The ship was sunk by the torpedoes dropped from a German bomber which scored direct hits on the munitions hold.

The explosion killed nine crew members and led to the rapid sinking of the ship which today lies at a depth of 30 metres. Remarkably well preserved, the wreck's cargo is still in place, with a number of railway wagons still anchored on the upper deck and two tanks clearly visible.

The hold contains trucks, cars, motorcycles, arms and ammunition.

97
The hull of the Thistlegorm *today lies at a depth of 30 metres and, as can be seen here, is still in admirable condition, making this a favourite site with experienced divers.*

98-99
Soft corals and sponges have colonised the wreck of the Thistlegorm *in spectacular fashion and the vessel is also home to schools of anthias.*

96-97 and 96 bottom
The sighting of a wreck is not unusual in the Red Sea, not even when diving off the coast of Sharm el-Sheikh, an area made perilous by the sharp emergent reefs. The Thistlegorm *was instead sunk in 1941 by the torpedoes of a German bomber which scored a direct hit on the vessel's ammunition store.*

From Suez to St. Catherine's

It is still possible to trace the route followed by Moses and his people during the biblical Exodus in search of the promised land, although it remains to be demonstrated just how closely the sites identified along this itinerary from Suez to St. Catherine's Monastery, or if you prefer from the Springs of Moses to Mount Sinai, correspond historically to the sites actually visited by him. As mentioned earlier, the most recent research suggests that the actual route taken by the Hebrews fleeing from Egypt was further to the north and avoided the heart of the Sinai and Gebel Musa. Whatever the historical truth may be, the magic of an itinerary that is nonetheless described in the Bible in considerable detail remains in the hearts and expectations of visitors and is, as well as a geographical excursion, a true journey through western religious consciousness, a spiritual journey in search of emotions far from the frenzy of everyday life, along sandy tracks where time appears to have stood still. An experience, in short, of a pre-eminently mystical and religious nature that has no need of scientific documentation. From this point of view, the arid, lunar appeal of the scenery to be explored, its mysterious silences, and the warm light of the sunsets, undoubtedly help to intensify that sense of inner depth and closeness to the absolute,

100 top
It is said that the biblical Exodus towards Gebel Musa began in the Suez region (this photo shows the Red Sea entrance to the canal).

100 bottom
The famous Springs of Moses (Fayun Musa in Arabic) where according to tradition Moses allowed his people to rest during the flight from Egypt.

100-101
The west coast of the Sinai, a combination of sea and desert.

101 bottom
The long strip of asphalt that links Suez with the south of the Sinai peninsula.

102-103
The interior of the Sinai in the vicinity of Wadi Feiran.

transmitted by these landscapes and the history attributed to them. Moreover, the itinerary includes visits to a number of other sites, some of them off the beaten tourist tracks and far removed from the biblical context, but equally interesting in historical and naturalistic terms.

From the subterranean tunnel of Ahmed Hamdi, which passes beneath the Suez canal, inaugurated in 1869, the route heads south for a number of kilometres as far as Oyun Musa, the Springs of Moses: this well, fed by a hot spring, is located on a hill, surrounded by rare palms and frequented for the most part by goats in search of food and water. These are supposedly the Springs of Marah reached by the people of Israel after three days' march from the Red Sea. The itinerary then proceeds along the coastal road while, on the right, the Red Sea expresses the blue and dark grey sides of its

nature. Crude oil tankers float off-shore and here and there shrines to the black gold can be seen on the orizon. Silos, pumping stations, pipelines that dive bravely into the sea, signs that testify to Egypt's role as an oil exporting country.

The city of Ras as-Sudr also developed thanks to oil, although its relative closeness to Suez and Cairo has made possible its partial conversion to tourism. A detour of around fifty kilometres to the south-east leads to Qalat al-Gindi, a citadel completed by Saladin in the twelfth century.

Having returned to the coastal road, our itinerary reaches El Gharandal on the banks of a wadi which in winter is characterised by rushing waters descending from the spectral limestone hills of the El 'Tih plateau, the geographical feature dominating central Sinai. According to the scriptures, the Exodus caravan also passed this way.

There follows Gebel Hammam Fara'un, a rock almost 500 metres high overlooking the Red Sea coast. Known as the "Bath of the Pharaoh", this mountain, which is reached by making a three-kilometre diversion along the coast, owes its name to a hot sulphur spring with therapeutic properties. This was the point where, in the Biblical account, the Egyptian soldiers chasing Moses were swallowed up by the Red Sea.

The main road heads into the uplands before returning to the coast to cross the Wadi Tayeba and reach Abu Zenima. A road heading west leads to the temple of Serabit el-Khadim, located on the summit of a hill that, after fifty kilometres on

104 top
This Bedouin cemetery is located close to the ancient mining site of Bir Nasib.

104 bottom
The Nawamis ("Flies" in Arabic) complex, a group of dry-stone tombs, is situated along the road from Dahab to St. Catherine's.

104-105
Wadi Arada Hakatan is a geological marvel with coloured rocks and calcareous erosions.

105 bottom
The ruins of ancient Pelusium extend over a vast area on the edge of the delta.

106-107
The suggestive natural architecture of the Forest of Columns at Gebel Fuga.

mainly asphalted roads, requires an extra three-quarters of an hour for the final climb on foot. The temple is dedicated to Hathor, the goddess of turquoise, and was intended to protect the mines in the area which was also rich in copper. Among the dozens of stelae from the Middle and New Kingdoms, of particular note are those dedicated to Hatshepsut and Thutmosis III.

There is an interesting excursion from this area to the spectacular canyon known as the Giants' Gorge which progressively narrows to the point where only one vehicle may pass at a time. Here, at various times of the day, the sun creates plays of light and shadow, modifying the chromatic graduation of the warm-tone rock according to its height in the sky. Sculpted by the eroding forces of the wind and the sand, the rock has taken on fantastic shapes and the traveller's gaze is captured by a natural kaleidoscope of forms and colours. In order to reach the true turquoise mines, one again has to return to the coast and reach Abu Rudeis, located 165 kilometres from the tunnel below the canal. A track heading west leads to Wadi Sidri and, after a 22-kilometre hike, to the slopes of Gebel Atairtir el Dahmi. Here are the entrances to the mines of Maghara, excavated and exploited in the eras of Snefru and Cheops, the great pharaohs of the fourth dynasty; a number of inscriptions on stelae dedicated to the ancient monarchs mark the entrance to the mines.

The road that heads inland from Abu Rudeis towards St. Catherine's encounters, roughly mid-way between the Red Sea and the monastery, the delicious, fresh and brilliantly green oasis of El-Feiran, located at the foot of Gerbel Serbal (2,070 metres). Tradition has it that the biblical Redifim,

the Hebrews' last encampment before Mount Sinai was sited here. It was anything but a tranquil stop and the area at that time was probably not as rich in water: the thirsty people protested against Moses who in reply smote the rock indicated by God with his rod to allow water to flow. Moreover, the Hebrews were attacked by the Amaleks, eventually winning the first battle in their history.

Nothing of this tumultuous climate is evoked by this splash of green palms and tamarisks today, four square kilometres of fertile land on which cereals, fruit and of course dates are cultivated. The roughly 650 Bedouins who live here in mud huts also raise livestock.

Beyond Feiran, the scenery through which the road to St. Catherine's passes changes frequently, presenting the drama of sheer granite canyons, the bottleneck of El Bab, the door, which gives access to the lunar valley of Wadi el Sheik, whose peaks present shimmering colours that range from green through to red and black. Beyond the Watia pass comes the immense Er-Raha plain. Here the Hebrews are said to have pitched the camp from which Moses departed alone in the direction of Gebel Musa and it was here, or more precisely on Gebel Harun, where a mosque now stands, that the people of Israel, exhausted by their wait, erected the golden calf. St. Catherine's is now just around the corner.

108 bottom
Numerous bas-reliefs adorn the chapel dedicated to Hathor in the temple at Serabit el-Khadim.

108-109
A panoramic view of the Serabit el-Khadim temple in the Sinai desert.

109 bottom
The temple at Serabit el-Khadim is located in an area rich in mineral resources. The turquoise mines justified intensive exploitation by the pharaohs of the 12th dynasty who promoted the erection of the temple. The building was initially dedicated to Hathor, the "Goddess of Turquoise".

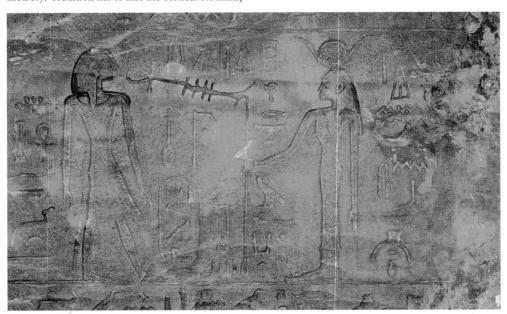

110-111
A magnificent expanse of
palm trees, the largest in the
whole of the Sinai,
characterises El Feiran
Oasis, situated along the
wadi of the same name.

110 bottom
The nuns' convent (on the
left, one of the two ancient
bells, on the right, the
entrance portal) found in
the Wadi Feiran is
subordinate to St.
Catherine's Monastery.
Many of the monastery's
architectural features come
from buildings erected in
this valley from the 4th
century onwards.

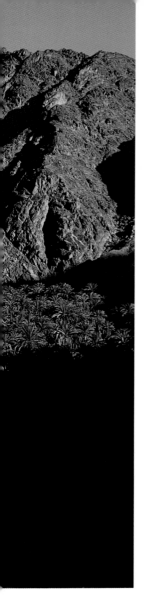

111

It is surprising how much vegetation is to be found in the vicinity of the monastery: small plots of palms, acacias, tamarisks and grapefruit trees. The verdant Wadi Feiran links the coastline of the Gulf of Suez with St. Catherine's. It was here that, according to the Bible, the battle was fought between the Hebrews led by Joshua and the Amaleks, a sedentary tribe.

112 top
The mausoleum of Sheikh Harun stands on the el-Raha plain, also known as the Plain of Rest as here, according to tradition, the Hebrews pitched camp and saw the sacred mountain for the first time. Alongside the mausoleum is the Chapel of the Golden Calf.

112 bottom left
A small clearing between St. Catherine's Monastery and Mount Sinai is known as the Amphitheatre of the Seventy Elders of Israel. It was here, the Bible says, the elders who accompanied Moses had to remain.

112 bottom right
The tomb of a Bedouin
chieftain decorated with the
traditional coloured fabric.

112-113
Not far from St.
Catherine's stands the sober
Bedouin cemetery of
Feiran.

113 bottom
The rugged mountains of
the Sinai massif surround
the Feiran Oasis.

St. Catherine's Monastery

The origins of St. Catherine's Monastery lie
back in the fourth century: historical sources cite
324 as the year in which this valley was settled by
a community of monks who asked Empress
Helena, the mother of the emperor Constantine,
permission to build a chapel on the site in which
they claimed to have identified the burning bush.
The chapel financed by Helena was completed in
334. Two centuries later, the structure was
extended, thanks to the intervention of the
Roman emperor Justinian, and protected by the
massive enclosure wall that, renders the complex
more akin to a fortress than a religious building.
The monastery was finally completed in 565. But
why St. Catherine's? The body of a nun, martyred
in the fourth century at Alexandria in Egypt at the
behest of the tetrarch Maximian, is said to have
been transported by an angel to the area of Mount
Sinai where it was discovered between the seventh
and ninth centuries. The remains were
recomposed in the monastery where they still lie.
The complex has been violated only once during
its millennial history, in the 7th century. Tradition
has it that Mohamed in person granted the monks
his protection in 625. The monks' gratitude to
him was shown through the construction of a
mosque within the complex.

*Market gardens and
orchards are located outside
the enclosure walls built
during the age of Justinian:
great cypresses, olives and
fruit trees supply the
necessary shade.*

116 top
A powerful enclosure wall in red granite surrounds the monastery; its height varies from 9 to 15 metres, while at certain points it is over 2 metres thick.

116 bottom
A number of buildings are grouped within the enclosure wall, including the celebrated library, the museum and the icon gallery, the refectory and the monks' cells (on the right the doorway to the cells inside the monastery).

St. Catherine's has through history thus remained an oasis of peace, spared not only by its isolation, but also by the aura of mystery and sacredness that surrounds it. When, in the eighth century, emperor Leo III ordered the destruction of all religious images in the Christian communities, the monastery's works of art were the only ones to survive. Not even the crusades left any trace, except for the graffiti incised by the Christian troops in the ancient refectory. The development of the complex in that period is demonstrated by the figures regarding the number of monks living there: 40 in the tenth century (together with 30 nuns and a staff of 100 lay persons) and 100 (with 50 nuns) in the twelfth and thirteenth centuries, when the basilica of St. Helena was built.

Protected and financed by the emperor Frederick Barbarossa, the monastery was equipped with a more robust enclosure wall with no doorways. From then onwards access to the interior of the complex was by way of a robust net, similar to an enormous shopping bag, lowered and raised by a winch. The earthquake of 1312 interrupted the monastery's tranquil life: only the massive external walls and the precious library survived. The reconstruction of the monastery was completed in 1461. In 1483, Saint Fabrizio died here after arriving the previous year at the end of a 32-year crossing of the Sinai desert on foot. His remains still rest at St. Catherine's. Subsequently, St. Catherine's only managed to escape the Ottoman assault thanks to the intercession of the orthodox Pope of Mount Athos and the intervention of the Russian empress Catherine the Great.

In exchange, the abbot of St. Catherine's placed the complex under the jurisdiction of the monks of Mount Athos, a situation that is unchanged today. The monastery then came under British protection and later retained its autonomy and independence with respect to the new Egyptian state. It was the foundation of Israel and the occupation of Sinai between 1967 and 1982 that created a situation of isolation. With the restitution of Sinai to Egypt and the gradual resolution of the Middle East conflict, St. Catherine's was then to become the objective of increasingly frequent tourist pilgrimages. The visit of Pope John Paul II in 2000 conferred further prestige upon the complex.

118 top left and 119
The Basilica's interior, richly decorated with comitless lamps hanging from the ceiling, it is dominated by a

large wooden icon holder from the 17th century, showing Christ, the Virgin Mary, and some saints - one of them Catherine.

118 top right
The Byzantine-style three-naved basilica dates back to 527 AD.

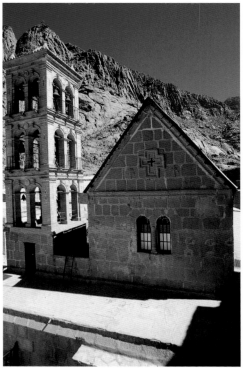

Still today St. Catherine's Monastery resembles more a powerful fortress than a place of faith, enclosed as it is within its inaccessible walls, overlooked by corner towers, surrounded by an internal walkway up to three metres thick and between eight and twenty-five metres high. Today, there is an entrance, close to which the winch which once guaranteed access can be seen. Outside the monastery, a small hostel offers board and lodgings while the inside (covering an area of 6,000 m²) resembles a Medieval village: a labyrinth of alleys, arches, passages and corridors jumbled almost one on top of another, the whole overlooked by a campanile and a minaret. Only a small part of St. Catherine's is open to the public. The treasures it conserves are too precious to allow access to a library containing thousands of works of immense value, including ancient manuscripts that are testimony to early Christianity. Up until the last century, the library, which is second only to that of the Vatican in number and value of its volumes, also conserved the Codex Sinaiticus, a manuscript from the late fourth century which is a copy of the Greek original of the New and Old Testaments.

118 centre
The apse of the basilica, adorned by the splendours of the Mosaic of the Transfiguration.

118 bottom
The Icon Gallery, an annexe to the library, boasts over 2,000 paintings.

The refectory is currently closed for renovation, the well of Moses is covered up. Even the Basilica conceals its most precious treasure from the public: the 6th century mosaic of the transfiguration that decorates the apse. It resembles the mosaic of Istanbul's Hagia Sophia, and depicts Christ flanked by Moses and Elijah, with the apostles Peter, James and John kneeling at his feet. Obscuring the view of the mosaic, and preventing access to the Chapel of the Burning Bush, is the iconostasis typical of Orthodox churches, composed of four panels in gilded and inlaid wood framing the icons of Christ, Mary, St. Catherine and St. John the Baptist. In the absence of an accommodating monk, you are left to admire the general structure of the basilica: it is by no means a large church (40 metres by 20), but is nonetheless impressive with its three naves divided by granite colonnades, the glowing light provided by the dozens of wax lanterns hanging from the sixteenth century wooden ceiling and lastly the splendid portal said to date from the era of Justinian. Composed of twenty-eight inlaid panels the door was made either from cedar of Lebanon or cypress wood. The narthex, a vestibule preceding the main body of the church, contains an important collection of icons dating from the fifth to the seventh centuries, the only examples in the world to be spared during the

iconoclastic wars. Anothers 150, are conserved in the complex's picture gallery: these date from the fifth to the fifteenth centuries and reflect the Byzantine history by way of an artistic itinerary from the early Christian works, characterised by extensive use of gold and sacred portraits via local Coptic art, to the middle Ages with pre-Renaissance tendencies. Although the great picture gallery is not open to the public, outside the church, in the apsidal area that reveals the location of the chapel of the burning bush, you can see what is said to be the actual bush that burst into flames before Moses' eyes and has survived intact to this day. The bush was replanted here to allow the construction of the altar in the tiny chapel above its roots. Before leaving St. Catherine's you should look back to see the complex in its entirety and to perceive the closeness and harmony of the simple Christian campanile and the minaret of the minuscule mosque. Only our memory and enthusiasm will, in fact, be able to transmit the atmosphere of these scenes to family and friends, the chromatic appeal of these icons, the subtle ochre of the buildings the severe but ironic expressions of the monks laughing under their beards at the naive wonder of the tourists and their wide-open eyes when it is explained to them that no photography is allowed at St. Catherine's.

121

The ancient icons conserved at St. Catherine's embellish the narthex of the basilica and the famous Icon Gallery. They were created by the monks, mostly between the 10th and 15th centuries, and are the expression of an original and sophisticated art form. At the top can be seen a Madonna and Child, while at the bottom is the celebrated Stairway to Heaven of St. John of the Cross.

On foot up the Gebel Musa

The climb from the 1,570 metres a.s.l. of St. Catherine's Monastery to the 2,285 of the summit of Gebel Musa is a heavy two and a half hour trek, especially in the last section. The best period to go is in spring and autumn, but summer is feasible too. The only precautions needed are adequate protection from the sun and wind-proof jackets to wear over your sweat-soaked clothing once you

have reached the top. The ideal programme is to depart around mid-afternoon, watch the sunset and bivouac on the summit so as to awaken with the first rays of the new day. Should you decide to descend after sunset or to climb before dawn you will need a good torch, but of equal importance is your choice of route. There are, in fact, two footpaths linking St. Catherine's with the summit: in the dark it is imperative that you take the mule track with gentle curves that during the day can even be covered on the back of a camel. More demanding, but decidedly more attractive is the Skikkat Satna Musa, that is to say the "Path of Moses": four thousand irregular steps, perhaps carved into the rock by a penitent monk.

Having completed the first section, you proceed along tight, narrow gorges of unique appeal. The path is marked by a number of religious buildings, beginning with the Chapel of the Virgin Mary, which is followed by the Confession Gate, a stone arch over the path that indicates the place where the pilgrims would once ask a monk forgiveness for their sins. If the indulgence was not granted the trek ended here. A second arch, St. Stephen's Gate, precedes a clearing with cypresses, an enclosure wall and a precious pool of water. The summit is not far from here, but the going now gets even tougher. Beyond the junction between the stepped footpath and the mule track, there are seven hundred steep steps that climb to the peak. Hence the first Bedouins, strategically positioned to await the tourist-trekkers in order to offer them hot tea, biscuits and drinks, or blankets for those who wish to spend the night at the top. As you look up towards the nearing summit, you will see the silhouette of a small apse: this is the Chapel of the' Holy Trinity, built in 1934 on the ruins of an earlier building, which flanks a small mosque.

The two buildings are symbols of two of the three religions that believe in a single god; two monuments erected on the very spot in which monotheism was sanctioned in the Tablets of the Law given to Moses.

122 top
The Confession Gate along the steps climbing Gebel Musa or Mount Moses.

122 bottom
The tiny Chapel of the Holy Trinity at the top of Mount Moses.

122-123

*The warm tones of dawn
are reflected on the
mountains surrounding the
peak of Gebel Musa.*

123 bottom

*St. Catherine's Monastery
is photographed here from
the footpath that leads to
Mount Moses.*

Central Sinai and Mt. St. Catherine

Central Sinai not only offers the historical and mystical appeal of St. Catherine's Monastery or Gebel Musa. Its high plains, its wind-carved gorges, the oases, the dry river beds, the warm tones of the rocks all contribute to a natural spectacle of incomparable beauty, one to be discovered during an exploration that may last for several days. The base for these excursions is usually Sharm el-Sheikh, from where you may depart for El-Tur and then Wadi Feiran and Wadi Mukattab, following the east coast road. Alternatively, you can head east along the coast towards Dahab and Nuweiba, before penetrating to the heart of the peninsula and reaching the oases to the north-east of St. Catherine's.

The two routes also intersect behind St. Catherine's Monastery. The itinerary heading eastwards is generally the preferred option, as it offers the opportunity of visiting extremely interesting oases and wadis. Four-wheel drive vehicles are indispensable to tackle the sandy tracks along the route, as is comprehensive camping gear, given that the Sinai interior offers little in the way of accommodation.

The first stage takes us to Wadi Kheresa, where you can admire extensive mangrove swamps – the

124 top
The asphalted road that links Nuweisa and St. Catherine's passes through landscapes of great beauty, dominated by limestone and sandstone outcrops of warm, golden tones.

124 bottom
Sculpted by the erosive power of the wind, remarkable rock formations can be seen along the road to St. Catherine's.

124-125
Gebel Katherina which reaches an altitude of 2,642 metres, is the highest peak in the Sinai.

125 bottom
Low tamarisks, the so-called "trees of manna", resist the oppressive heat of the desert around St. Catherine's. Here we are on the slopes of Uadi Ghazala, the "Valley of the Gazelles".

mangroves are aquatic plants capable of surviving in a saline environment. Proceeding inland, you cross the Wadi Kid and the Wadi Madsula, dry river beds enclosed amidst spectacular and grandiose granite mountains.

Having passed Bir Nasb and heading westwards, the itinerary reaches St. Catherine's Monastery and Gebel Musa. At this point you can take in the climb to the Sinai's highest peak, not Moses' Mount Sinai, but rather Gebel Katherina which reaches a height of 2,342 metres. Here the angels are said to have taken the body of St. Catherine after she had been martyred in Alexandria. It takes about five hours to reach the summit, but it is worth the effort for the unique view, especially on a clear day. In any case you will be able to see, beyond the lunar mountain landscape of the Sinai, the gulfs of Suez

and Aqaba, which are in turn framed by the mountains of Africa and Arabia. At the top of the mountain a two-roomed construction provides shelter for the excursionists.

From the asphalted road that leads to the monastery it is possible to reach another of the Sinai's marvels. This is the Blue Desert, a plateau on which, in 1981, the Belgian artist Jean Verame celebrated the end of the war between Egypt and Israel by painting numerous rocky outcrops in deep blue, a symbol of peace. The performance required the use of 10 tonnes of paint and was at the centre of heated debates. In any case, the Blue Desert, thanks to the surreal colouring of its rocks, in sharp contrast with the ochre tones of the desert, has an unforgettable visual impact that makes a visit worthwhile.

126

The dazzling, lunar appeal of the Blue Desert: the reflections of the uniquely coloured rocks contrast sharply with the ochre desert. It was the Belgian artist Jean Verame who, between 1980 and 1981, painted the rocks on a plateau a few kilometres from St. Catherine's blue in order to celebrate peace between Egypt and Israel.

126-127
Jean Verame used almost ten tones of paint in his performance.

127 bottom
A Bedouin awaits the arrival of the tourists on the tallest of the blue rocks.

128-129
The oasis of Ain, Umm Ahmed is one of the Sinai's most beautiful, thanks to the usually plentiful supply of water which favours the growth of palms and tamarisks.

130 top
This rocky peak announces the vicinity of Wadi Mukattab, also known as the Valley of the Inscriptions due to the numerous graffiti found here.

130 bottom
The Wadi Arada Hakatan reveals the typical sandy bed along which water once ran.

131
The oasis of Ain Khudra, photographed here from above, stands on the course of the wadi of the same name and is characterised by unusually light sandstone and limestone outcrops.

Returning to the asphalted road that departs from the monastery, you can choose whether to head west in the direction of Wadi Feiran, or east towards Nuweiba. In the first case you trace in reverse part of the Exodus route described earlier. Having reached the coast you can turn south and head back to Sharm el-Sheikh. Along the Wadi Feiran it is worth taking a diversion to the north-west that leads in just a few kilometres to Wadi Mukattab. The sandstone walls of this valley, orphaned of its now dry river, carry graffiti in the Nabataean idiom, inscriptions from the prehistoric era and other writings in the Aramaic, Sephardic, Hebrew and Greek languages.

In the second case, that is to say, heading towards Nuweiba and taking several unpaved side tracks, you will have the opportunity to enjoy a number of enchanting sights.

Having passed the necropolis of Nawamis, you can deviate in the direction of Ain Khudra, where there are natural springs preceding the Oasis of Ain Umm Ahmed (the "Spring of the Mother of Ahmed"), one of the most beautiful and most extensive in the Sinai. Infrequently visited, and perhaps for this reason particularly suggestive, the oasis of Ain Umm Ahmed is a vast palm grove, interrupted by small cultivated patches where the Bedouins grow fruit and market vegetables.

From Ain Umm Ahmed you can head into the fantastic landscape of the Wadi Ghazala, the Valley of the Gazelles, dominated by red sandstone walls alternating with sandy plains.

This ancient river bed owes its name to the once very numerous population of these typical desert ungulates.

On the far side of a pass is the oasis of Ain Hudra, embraced by mountains that form a grandiose natural amphitheatre. A path through the gorges cutting into these mountains allows you to see walls of stratified rocks of different colours.

Since the earliest times, Bedouin tribes have camped around the well in the oasis of Ain Hudra, as testified by the numerous rock engravings to be found in the area. A characteristic element of the landscape in this part of the Sinai is the geological composition of the rocks which alternate from red sandstone to marble-like white limestone, at times split by basalt dykes.

The presence of ferrous and manganese oxides in the sandstone accentuates the variety of colours. The result is spectacular: the long tracks, almost always along the sandy wadis, far from the flat monochromatic desert, offer surprising tints. Equally stunning is the appearance of certain rock formations that due to the friability of the minerals and the particularly erosive effects of atmospheric agents take on the strangest of shapes.

A particularly attractive track is the one that heads towards the oasis of Ain Furtaga: panoramic and spectacular, it passes through geologically extraordinary landscapes rich in colour due to the different mineralogical compositions of the surrounding rocks.

Beyond the oasis of Ain Furtaga, an unpaved road leads to the Wadi Nekheill, and then to a plateau and to a steep path down into the valley.

132
The oasis of Ain Umm Ahmed (the "Spring of the Mother of Ahmed") owes its name to the extraordinarily plentiful water supply.

132 bottom
Two panoramic views of Wadis Arada Hakatan (left) and Mandar (right), along the road between Dahab and the St. Catherine's region.

133
Due to their mineral composition (rich in ferrous and manganese oxides) and the deterioration over the centuries caused by atmospheric agents, the sandstone rocks characteristic of this part of the Sinai can take on extraordinary colours and shapes.

This stunning effect becomes all the more fascinating as the walls increase in height to a notable maximum of around a hundred metres, that is to say the equivalent of an immense natural skyscraper. The walk through the canyon presents no particular difficulties and the easy going allows you to linger over the natural beauties of the area and stop to take photographs. As you leave you will be left with the strong sensation of having experienced an adventure of rare intensity.

At least brief mention should be made of the so-called "lithic inscriptions" that are fairly common in central Sinai and may be observed by making only brief deviations from the itineraries described. There are three particularly well known sites. The Wadi Mukattab, whose name actually translates as the "Valley of the Inscriptions", was mentioned earlier. The Rock of the Inscriptions (Haggar Muktab, the "Written Stone", as it is known to the locals), can be reached along an easy track off the Nuweiba-St. Catherine's road and features graffiti from the

134
The Coloured Canyon owes its name to the infinite variations in tone created by the minerals contained in the sandstone into which it was carved by the action of water during the Quaternary period. Similar geological formations can be found not far from the Sinai, in the vicinity of the city of Petra, in Jordan.

135 top
The Coloured Canyon narrows gradually until it becomes a narrow cleft little wider than a metre in certain points.

135 bottom
Proceeding along the footpath, the towering sheer walls allow only a thin strip of sky to be seen.

From here on you should proceed along the canyon, ignoring the progressive narrowing of its walls. It is a narrow gorge with steep ochre walls that, in the changing light, take on surprising tones made all the more attractive by the stratification that creates incredible lines and designs in the rock. This is the Coloured Canyon which thanks to its immense appeal is one of the most popular destinations in this part of the Sinai. Numerous daily excursions bring tourists here from the Nuweiba coast to allow them to discover this wonderful corner of uncontaminated, lunar landscape. Traversing the canyon requires around two hours and guarantees a sequence of remarkable sights thanks to the variety of geological formations that create remarkable shapes and colour variations, in part a result of the passage of water that has over the centuries traced furrows and stripes of changing tones, culminating in an intense ochre. Every now and then, you should glance upwards to where the summits of the rocks appear very close together, allowing the blue of the sky to filter through a mere crack.

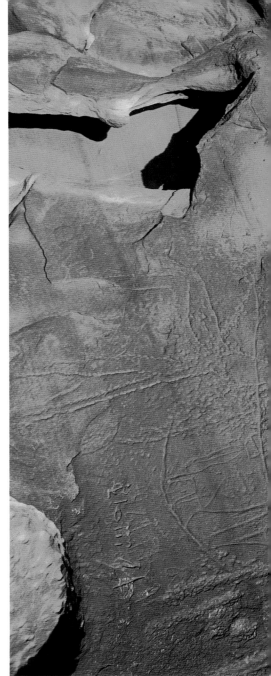

Nabataean, Roman and Byzantine ages.

The Serabit el-Khadim site and the surrounding area instead feature hieroglyphic inscriptions from the Middle and New Kingdoms (among the largest stele is one dating from the reign of Sethos I), with religious formulas and accounts of mineral expeditions, along with stunning mysterious graffiti such as those of Rod el-Air (the "Valley of the Donkeys" named after the beasts of burden that carried the tonnes of turquoise extracted from the pharaohs' mines), depicting Nile boats in a desert-like area hundreds of kilometres from the river.

136 top and 137 bottom
On the rock walls at Rod el-Air, numerous inscriptions have been found, some of which depict a number of boats. It remains a mystery why such a desert environment the ancient artist felt the urge to portray such typically Nilotic scenes.

136 bottom
The wadi at Rod el-Air, around a kilometre and a half west of the track that leads to Serabit el-Khadim, was the site of the last encampment before the ascent to the temple plateau. According to the archaeologists, this is demonstrated by numerous remains of ancient camps and the hieroglyphs found here.

136-137
The rocks surrounding the wadi take on a strong reddish colouring at dusk. The appeal of this region is remarkable, despite the Arab name which translates as "Valley of the Donkeys", a tribute to the animals used by the caravans heading to and from the turquoise mines.

138-139
A Bedouin acts as a guide, indicating the rock inscriptions.

140-141
Wadi Mukattab, a place name that means the "Valley of the Inscriptions", is adorned with numerous graffiti, mostly from the Nabataean age although some are of Greco-Roman and Byzantine origins.